Three Ballplayers

by Greg Rogers

Scott Foresman
is an imprint of

Glenview, Illinois • Boston, Massachusetts • Chandler, Arizona
Upper Saddle River, New Jersey

Every effort has been made to secure permission and provide appropriate credit for photographic material. The publisher deeply regrets any omission and pledges to correct errors called to its attention in subsequent editions.

Unless otherwise acknowledged, all photographs are the property of Scott Foresman, a division of Pearson Education.

Photo locators denoted as follows: Top (T), Center (C), Bottom (B), Left (L), Right (R), Background (Bkgd)

Opener: Baseball Hall of Fame Library, Cooperstown, NY; 1 Getty Images; 3 (T) Bettmann/Corbis, (BR) Getty Images; 4 (Bkgd) Getty Images, (CL) Brand X Pictures, (BC) Baseball Hall of Fame Library, Cooperstown, NY; 5 Baseball Hall of Fame Library, Cooperstown, NY; 6 Getty Images; 7 (CR) Getty Images, (BC) Baseball Hall of Fame Library, Cooperstown, NY; 8 (Bkgd) Getty Images, (BC) Baseball Hall of Fame Library, Cooperstown, NY; 9 (CR) © Comstock Inc., (B) Baseball Hall of Fame Library, Cooperstown, NY; 10 (Bkgd) Getty Images, (B) © Bettmann/Corbis; 11 (CR) Brand X Pictures, (B) Baseball Hall of Fame Library, Cooperstown, NY; 12 (Bkgd) Getty Images, (B) George Strock/Getty Images

ISBN 13: 978-0-328-51330-7
ISBN 10:   0-328-51330-X

Copyright © by Pearson Education, Inc., or its affiliates. All rights reserved.
Printed in the United States of America. This publication is protected by copyright, and permission should be obtained from the publisher prior to any prohibited reproduction, storage in a retrieval system, or transmission in any form or by any means, electronic, mechanical, photocopying, recording, or likewise. For information regarding permissions, write to Pearson Curriculum Rights & Permissions, One Lake Street, Upper Saddle River, New Jersey 07458.

Pearson® is a trademark, in the U.S. and/or in other countries, of Pearson plc or its affiliates.

Scott Foresman® is a trademark, in the U.S. and/or in other countries, of Pearson Education, Inc., or its affiliates.

3 4 5 6 7 8 9 10 V0N4 13 12 11 10

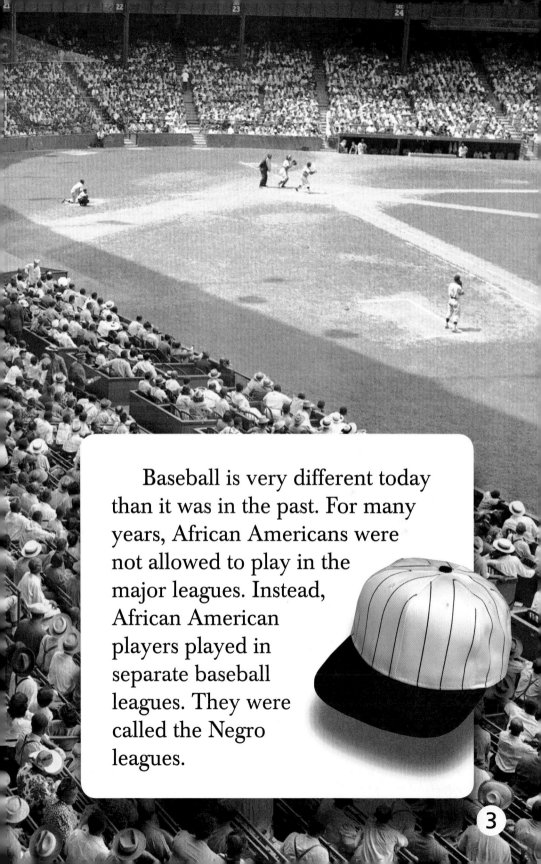

Baseball is very different today than it was in the past. For many years, African Americans were not allowed to play in the major leagues. Instead, African American players played in separate baseball leagues. They were called the Negro leagues.

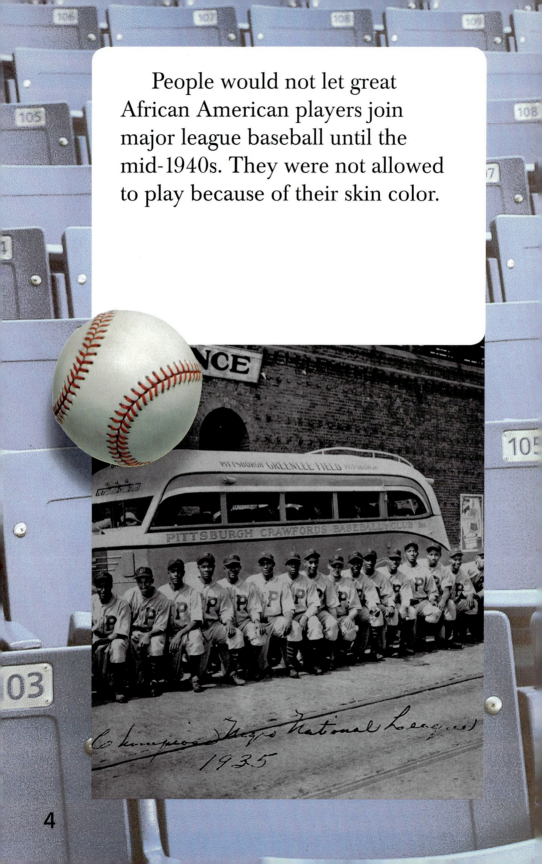

People would not let great African American players join major league baseball until the mid-1940s. They were not allowed to play because of their skin color.

Amazing Pitcher Satchel Paige

Satchel Paige played in the Negro leagues. He threw a baseball with great control. He could trick any hitter at the plate. Satchel Paige pitched and enjoyed the cheers of fans for more than twenty years.

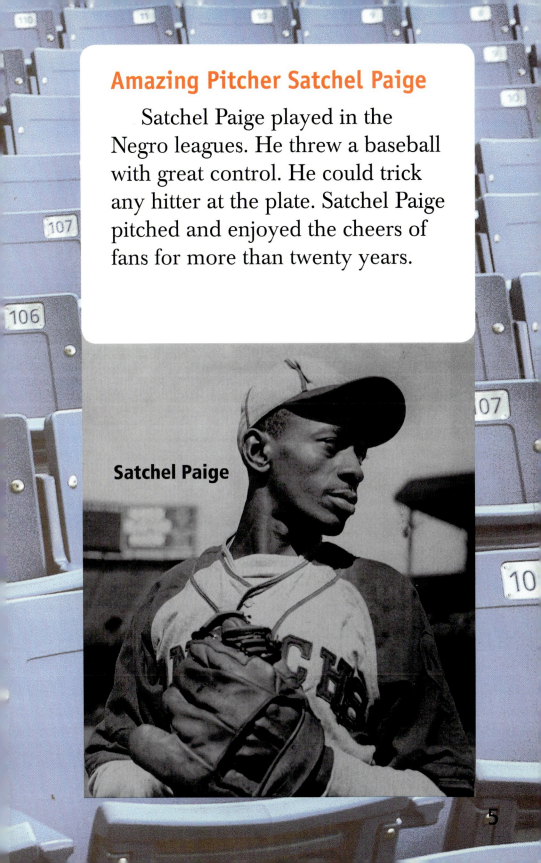

Satchel Paige

In the 1940s some African American players were finally asked to join the major leagues. Paige joined the Cleveland Indians. His pitching helped the Indians win the 1948 World Series.

Satchel Paige

Flyball Chaser Cool Papa Bell

James "Cool Papa" Bell was known for his speed in running around the bases. For thirty years Cool Papa Bell was called the fastest man in baseball.

James Bell

Cool Papa Bell sailed across the field. People joked that he ran so fast he could turn off the lights and be in bed before they went out! Cool Papa Bell entered the Baseball Hall of Fame in 1974.

James Bell

Power Hitter Josh Gibson

Josh Gibson was best known for his batting skill. Some think he may be the greatest home run hitter in history. Some of Josh Gibson's home runs are still famous today.

Josh Gibson

Josh Gibson once hit a home run in Pittsburgh. The next day a ball landed in a ballpark in Philadelphia. It was more than two hundred miles away. People joked and said it must have been Gibson's hit from the day before!

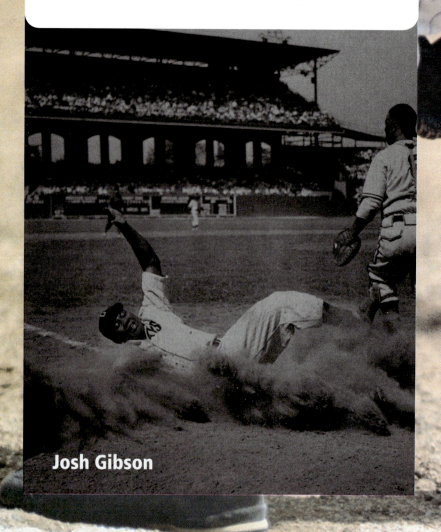

Josh Gibson

Josh Gibson played in the Negro leagues for seventeen years. He hit almost eight hundred home runs. Josh Gibson joined the Baseball Hall of Fame in 1972.

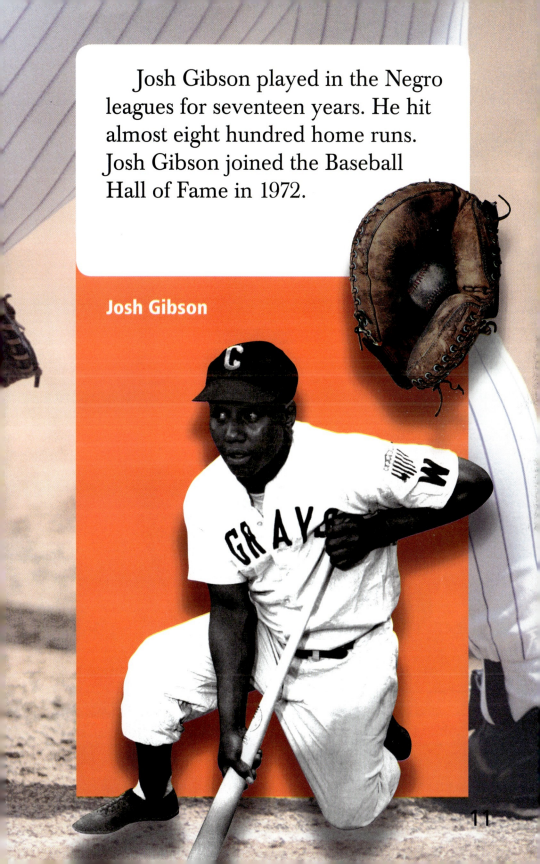

Josh Gibson

These three great ballplayers were kept out of the major leagues for many years. They were left out because of the color of their skin. This was not fair. Their amazing skill showed that they belonged with the best. Today they are all in the Baseball Hall of Fame.

Satchel Paige